SOMETIMES I FEEL LIKE A MOTHERLESS CHILD

Poems on the Global Black Experience

LAWRENCE MDUDUZI NDLOVU

African Perspectives Publishing
PO Box 95342, Grant Park 2051,
Johannesburg, South Africa
www.africanperspectives.co.za

© Lawrence Mduduzi Ndlovu 2024

All rights reserved

No part of this publication may be reproduced, stored in a retrieval system or transmitted in any form or by any means, electronic, mechanical, photocopying or otherwise,
without the prior permission of the author.

ISBN PRINT: 978-0-7961-7391-1
ISBN DIGITAL: 978-0-7961-7392-8

Editor (Poetry): Raphael d' Abdon
Editor (Text): Richard Gibbs
Proofreader: Rose Francis
Typesetter: Phumzile Mondlani
Cover Image: Eli Weinburg - Gallo Images
Cover Design: Jenilee Prinsloo - Ryzenberg

CONTENTS

PREFACE	vii
FOREWORD	xi
AFRICA	1
SCRAMBLE FOR AFRICA	3
SOPHIATOWN	5
ETERNALLY OWED	7
THERE IS A COST	10
CONGO FREE STATE	12
NATIVE LABOUR CORPS: SS MENDI	15
WE SPEAK THEIR LANGUAGE	18
GOD	19
BLACK BODIES	20
TAKE ME TO THE FRONTLINE STATES	22
VICTORY TROPHIES FOR INVADERS	24
MAMA-GIRL	26
DON'T YOU TAKE THAT BOW	28
THOSE TAKEN	31
MY BABY GIRL	33
RHINELAND BASTARDS	47
FOR SARAH BAARTMAN	49

TULSA	53
ANTI-BLACK PHILOSOPHERS	56
BRING HIM HOME	58
TODAY	61
EVEN UNSAID IT STILL IS	63
COLOURISM	65
BAN THE BLACK MAN	66
AMERICA	68
FLOYD	70
UKRAINE	72
THE BEAUTIFUL GAME	73
BLACK THUG	74
COVID: THEY DIDN'T FORGET	76
REFERENCES	79

DEDICATION

To the memory of Ambassador Lindiwe Mabuza, who with her lovely gaze could convince any person to believe in their own art

Where does brave steel go

When firmed foundations

Stood erect in crippling infirmity

Then blazed across furious skies

Sharply tracing revolution's flowers

With crimson tips

Along the rough edges of history

Say, where does brave steel go?

Lindiwe Mabuza

PREFACE

MEMORY AS KNOWLEDGE

My little niece is a wonder to experience. Her bright eyes are the window to a towering intellectual journey. She is a wordsmith, and her poetry suggests a depth of thought and emotional articulacy that is a marvel for such a young person. It was her aunt's birthday, and she had written a moving poem. All the adults in the room were spellbound by her words. I was proud and excited that she was in love with words.

As I think about her, I cannot help but think about how different her childhood is from mine. When I was born in 1984, South Africa was in the middle of a state of emergency, and *apartheid* was in full swing. When we eventually attained our political freedom in 1994, I was only ten years old. Thus far, I have spent my life having to negotiate and adjust to a racialised experience. My niece, on the other hand, does not have the burden of this memory.

This experience stirs up several thoughts about social memory and forgetfulness. To some degree, my niece represents the triumph of the struggle that was waged against *apartheid*. At the same time, she represents a particular success of the colonial project. She is fluent in English, her first language. But she is estranged from our cultural and tribal activities, and what is even harder to accept is the realisation that she might not have a very strong sense of Black pride because she has not been exposed to racial matters.

I realise that there are many other young people in the continent and in the African diaspora who are like my niece: they are experiencing a disconnection with the history and the experience of Black people around the world. They are fortunate they never experienced racism, but it is a worry that they do not know enough besides the messianic narratives of heroes and heroines who fought against a tyrannical system. I am not sure if they realise the scale of what has happened to us as Black people for centuries and how, up to this day, we are still negotiating a racialised experience.

The Challenges of a Compartmentalised Narrative

There is a danger in hastening to define racist incidents as isolated occurrences caused by evil individuals. It is a denial of racism being systemic and entrenched in the very lives and socialisations of persons in some communities.

Tied to this denialism is the tendency to compartmentalise single manifestations of racism and intentionally make no links with similar episodes happening daily on a global scale. It is very peculiar that a conversation about the evil of slavery can be held without any reference to colonialism, and yet they are both part of the same experience. It is the story of a single race – those who were taken and those who were left behind.

With the means at my disposal, I try to offer a broad view of what has happened to Black people everywhere. In doing this, I desire to assert that the evil imposed on Black people has been designed to consolidate the belief that we are inferior and that the heinous acts committed against us had underlining salvific connotations. To this day, some still argue that colonialism had its advantages or that descendants of enslaved people are lucky to end up where they are because African states have failed.

The Demand to Forgive and Forget

When conversations (reflections) are held on the Black experience, there is often a leap into forgiveness and forgetfulness. The actual acknowledgement of the crimes is not addressed; instead, it is suggested that the accepted behaviour should be normalised as a historical reality trapped in the past. However, the question remains: How do you tell the wounded that the war is over? How do you convince the victims still searching for answers that the matter is now closed? How do you persuade the wronged to forgive?

The notion of Black pain as something buried in the past fails to acknowledge the intergenerational trauma engraved in every Black person. Whether Black people have personally witnessed these "past" evils or not, they are still affected by them. While other nations make sure that the crimes committed against them are not obliterated, when it comes to Africans, we are expected to forget.

A Gaze at Ourselves

The above refers to outward-looking, but this book is also inward-looking. Those who have been and are still oppressed are hit by an acute sadness when they realise that their liberators seem to embody the cruelty typical of their oppressors. This work attempts to remind our leaders why they led African people to revolt against injustice; it also stresses how the bedrock of African liberation is rooted in the desire for equality and freedom for all people. It is shaped by the belief that we cannot replace racism with elitism and classism. Given our history, the existence of an African leadership oblivious to the Black agenda and not pursuing a Pan-Africanist agenda is absurd, even surreal.

I wrote this book for my niece, who must know her people's history and stories. It is also for those who innocently overlook the seriousness of racism and, limited by a narrow knowledge of this topic, lead a parochial existence. I hope their understanding will be broadened. I wrote this book for those who would like us to be silent about our pain. Finally, I wrote it for us –this is us.

Lawrence Mduduzi Ndlovu

FOREWORD

Chasing the Value of Memory and Forgiveness

Is memory our commitment to the past, an insistence to not forget, or the passing down of narratives through generations? Is it true knowledge or merely a collection of anecdotes? Throughout the corridors of this collection, these are the abiding questions which echo throughout. In a time when the struggle is between the responsibility of remembering and the danger of forgetting, we are called to conscientiousness. "Round them up, and let them join our ranks," Mduduzi Lawrence Ndlovu writes in these pages.

In this book, Mduduzi bottles the tension between memory and the forging of a future in the most delicate way. Mduduzi and I share a mother, although not an umbilical cord. We were both raised with love by Ambassador Lindiwe Mabuza, to whom this book is dedicated. An extraordinary human being who lived to see the seeds she planted blossom and then whither.

Through this collection of poems, Ndlovu not only boasts his exquisite talents as a writer but also gallantly attempts to remind us about what Lindiwe Mabuza and her comrades stood for and fought for. It also reminds us what is now at stake. What do our younger compatriots know, and how are they empowered by history?

While she walked the world, Lindiwe Mabuza never missed an opportunity to tell the truth, empower a young person, promote women, celebrate the arts and, most of all, lift the cause of freedom.

This book is also about the value of forgiveness. I use "value" to approximate gain – what is held or what could be lost. As South Africans, we have been reminded of what we risk losing if we do not forgive and why we must reconcile.

In my view, reconciliation implies there was once conciliation between Blacks and whites. But, apartheid separated us from our humanity, as white people and as Black people. The conciliation process we had to work on (and on which we are still working) is conciliation with the one humanity we both share.

As Desmond Tutu put it: "True reconciliation exposes the awfulness, the abuse, the pain, the degradation, the truth. It could even sometimes make things worse. It is a risky undertaking, but in the end, it is worthwhile because, in the end, dealing with the real situation helps to bring real healing. Spurious reconciliation can bring only spurious healing".

We must thus opt for the value in reconciliation – our humanity. And indeed, as Ndlovu argues, in line with Tutu: "In forgiving, people are not being asked to forget. On the contrary, it is important to remember so that we should not let such atrocities happen again".

This is why this book is important. It calls us to memory. We need to remember Sophiatown so that our governments never succumb to the temptation of careless removals and the breaking up of communities.

The story of Hamilton Naki has yet to be well known, even though it is part of the epic story of Chris Barnard and his contribution to advancing human civilisation. It reminds us of what we lost through colonisation, dispossession, and apartheid. Black assistant surgeon Hamilton Naki should have been lauded for his key role in the world's first heart transplant, but he wasn't. He worked alongside Barnard, but his name has been erased from history. This book calls us to that memory.

In thinking about Hamilton Naki, our progress and excellence in arts and culture and our rise in the sciences in this short period of freedom tell us what civilisation lost with the exclusion determined by racism. What could we have done with the land and couldn't do because we were denied ownership, enterprise and the franchise!

As we look ahead, this book highlights our role in fostering a new civilisation and how we can leapfrog humanity towards what was lost when opportunities for Black people were systematically denied. This is the forgiveness and the (re)conciliation we must pursue. Remembering what was lost to humanity and what we can still lose if we forget.

This is an important book because it allows us to tackle important issues about our history and envision a new story within that history. I wish you would feel the joy this book brought to me – page after page. I wish it would find a well-deserved place in our schools' syllabi and be used to enrich our much-needed public engagements and meaningful debates.

Xhanti Payi

AFRICA

Deep in our truth rivers are calling

In the meadows sounds are humming

Crack

Sigh

Whispers

The elements are talking

Under the trees elders are meeting

Day by day order is maintained

The soil is tilled

people are fed

There where the baby weeps

The elder raises the child heavenward

Alas a child is born

Life upon life

On and on the clans grow

Pilgrims greet
Asking
Praying
wishing health and rain upon each other
One of them is moody today
Healers pray to heaven, asking for answers
The one at one with herbs mixes and cooks
Years and years of remedy have kept them alive

The brave ones sharpen their spears
Prepare for protection
The people are safe

No altar of perfection is suggested here
People live for each other
As the sun marks the day
and the moon guards the night
This is the cradle for humankind

Life is Africa

SCRAMBLE FOR AFRICA

The absurd straight line on Namibia's side,

is a reminder of how brazen it was,

when they separated people

with the strike of a pen

Clawing

Claiming

Africa for themselves.

In Berlin they were to rage,

with their own hands

tear down the wall that separated

east and west.

Yet for Africa

man-made separations still remain.

A successful project,

because living here today

is a beast birthed from othering,

that hovers over so-called borders,

to the one from the north it says:

"This is your line"

To the one in the South:

"Those from the west will not pass here"

To those in the east:

"Those are not your people".

"The Scramble for Africa" is a term used to represent the twenty plus years where European powers conquered and divided the African continent. However, the formalisation of that process took place at the Berlin Conference in 1884-5, where thirteen European countries plus the United States met and agreed on how Africa was to be divided up, resulting in the General Act of the Berlin Conference.[1]

---

[1] Thomas Pakenham, *The Scramble for Africa* (London: Abacus Little Brown Book Group, 2015).

SOPHIATOWN

When I tell them that there once was Sophiatown,
they think it is place where the clouds look like candy,
where unicorns roam the streets,
where magic seems to exist.

When they ask me;
"Where exactly were you born?"
I tell them – "Sophiatown",
but I can't take them there.

Once in our real magic,
we rode the clouds laced with ordinary lives.
All of us,
preoccupied with living,
the beauty of just being human
was there.

Where is it then?
It was taken down and destroyed,
the homes that birthed us,

the magic of an ordinary life,

was destroyed when the forces came,

and removed all of us,

to separate us by race.

My home is now matter of fairy tales.

Once upon a time there existed Sophiatown.

The National Party passed the Native Resettlement Act, No 19 of 1954. This Act allowed them to remove Blacks from any area within and close to the magisterial district of Johannesburg. This act was used to remove Blacks from Sophiatown. On 9th February 1955, two thousand armed policemen were sent to Sophiatown where they forcefully removed 60 000 inhabitants. They also destroyed Sophiatown. From 1960 to 1983, the apartheid government forcibly moved 3.5 million black South Africans in one of the largest mass removals of people in modern history. Thousands of Coloureds, Blacks, and Indians were removed from areas classified for white occupation.[2]

---

[2] *Overcoming Apartheid, Building Democracy*, (2005), Michigan State University
https://overcomingapartheid.msu.edu/multimedia.php?kid=163-582-18 [accessed 17/02/2023].

ETERNALLY OWED

She couldn't be consoled
when she thought of him.
She couldn't be restrained
when sorrow ripped her bare.
The great sea was
too great to enter.
Just as ships rode the waves
as they approached the shore,
they floated away with him,
drifting into the unknown.

What a sight it was
when they held her back,
from hurling herself
into the sea.
She wept
Wept for her father.
Wept for women.
Cried for her friends,
who were taken.

She waited

watched

as ships returned,

and every night,

she returned home disappointed.

Every day,

she stood on the shore,

hoping,

waiting for her father's return

She roams the streets,

filling the roads,

laden with her belongings,

belonging nowhere

She lost her land as well.

The wanderers,

cannot offer libations,

on the graves of those

who remained with them,

when others were taken,

for home is no more.

They still weep

just to see

the graves of those taken,

just to kneel,

at the place

where death descended,

just to say

to the souls of the taken;

"We have come to take you home"³.

They still weep,

for they lost

those who shared their blood

and also lost their land.

---

³ This verse refers to Diana Ferrus's poem "I've come to take you home", which is widely believed to be responsible for the return of Sarah Baartman's remains to South Africa in 2002. https://socialjustice.sun.ac.za/downloads/events/2022-10-diana-ferrus-on-sarah.pdf.

THERE IS A COST

Wear those diadems,

decorate yourself,

they remind me of the father I never knew.

The train to the city,

took my father away for months,

to dig and descend

in the belly of the earth,

so you can wear a precious stone.

There was a price;

lost relationships,

estrangement from the place called home.

No wonder they found concubines,

in those hostels

they needed to be held tight.

Home is that lonely woman,

who tries to hold things together,

through a mixture of motherly magic,

and communal friendships.

She too is scared,

and wants some loving,

yet when he comes back,

Their arms are foreign to each other.

They've spent more time apart than together.

Life is laced with years of absence and labour.

When our parents come home,

they are too tired to notice

that we are growing.

There are no nights after supper by the fire,

where we can laugh and know each other -

we just grow.

CONGO FREE STATE

Hail him then -
Leopold your Belgian king,
as structures fill your homeland,
call him the Builder King.

Builder king?
He first apportioned himself the Congo,
then all within it he called his own,
Did I hear you say Builder King?
His trowel was a blade,
he mixed with blood, not water.
His spade dug no foundations
but graves.

Builder king you say?
If you dig his human-laced foundations,
you will find hole-filled skulls,
and limbs without bodies.
Are those traces of his pickaxe
and hand saw?

Builder king you insist?
Builders raise walls,
But his were erected with Congo's timber,
chasing rubber one black life at a time.
Show me his skyscrapers
I will show how he scraped the Congo

Builder king
Over millions of lives.
every brick he laid
is worth one black life.

Hail him then
Leopold your Builder King.

King Leopold II was the king of Belgium. He also known as the "Builder King". He called himself the "founder and sole owner" of the Congo Free State. Leopold ran the Congo by using his militia force called the *Force Publique*. He extracted ivory and natural rubber in the 1890s. He did this by forced labour from the native population to harvest and process rubber. His administration was characterised by brutality, which included torture, murder, kidnapping, and the amputation of the hands of men, women, and children when the quota of rubber was not met. It is a fact that the Congolese population declined significantly during Leopold's rule. The causes of the decline included epidemic disease, acts of violence committed by the regime, severe famine caused by the regime's actions, and a low birth rate during the worst of the Rubber Terror (in the period from 1896 to 1903).[4]

---

[4] Martin Ewans, *European Atrocity, African Catastrophe: Leopold II, the Congo Free State and Its Aftermath* (London: Routledge, 2002).

NATIVE LABOUR CORPS: SS MENDI

Commemorating the Centenary of the Sinking of the SS Mendi

Did these Isles dare a warrior to silence?
Tides that rose to quell the brave?
Did war rob the peace?
Or did settlers snare a nation's posterity?

The fog still, concealing sight,
a nation's destiny could not blight,
Rhythms of home bellowed within,
Ancestral war-cries in refrain persist.

These Isles dared to silence the warrior
They knew whose spirit they dared to bend
Countrymen's force bid even tide arise,
Ocean tide reaching, dancing and clashing
Retreating as if to gather strength,
Advancing, hurling, ululating
Bantu regiments in complete might.

Warriors saw death before them face,
Its stench, its definiteness their sights dared,
Yet even the heat raiding cool
Couldn't a people's heat overwhelm,
a people's spirit in gut blazed
for ancestors stood before them in embrace.

Even in death's advancing silence,
Circumstance willing a turn only to self,
Even then to each other they turned;
"Wooo mtaka baba! Woo mtaka ma!
Are you dead that you do not hear my voice?"

The living across Africa's shores retort;
We are not dead!
Nor the sound of your voice unheard,
Your voice heralded even to the future unknown,
Your lying down was rightly with glee,
Knowing your own will never chart
waters of wars unknown,
your own will in freedom's peace sail.

"On 21 February 1917, the SS Mendi was struck by another ship not far from the Isle of Wight and badly damaged. It sank. More than 600 South African men died. How did it come that hundreds of South African men — predominantly black, and some white — were sailing from Cape Town to Le Havre, France? Like many thousands of others from across the British Empire, they were travelling to support the war effort. Put simply, Britain and her allies were running out of people and supplies."[5]

---

[5] Baroness Lola Young, The hidden history of the sinking of the SS Mendi, (2014) *British Council* https://www.britishcouncil.org/voices-magazine/hidden-history-sinking-ss-mendi [accessed 20/10/2023].

WE SPEAK THEIR LANGUAGE

This is the success of our past rulers;

we cannot even speak without

their language on our lips.

GOD

I kneel to contemplate my Maker,

Yet all I see as I close my eyes,

Are images of a divine who looks like my oppressor,

I cannot even pray,

Without the white gaze.

BLACK BODIES

These breasts
were never a sexual tool,
nor short skirts
a sexy suggestion.
This use of sex as power
was never our language.

His member was never a weapon,
his abs not a canvas for splendour,
his strength never just for battering.
Somehow human bodies were as ordinary
as everyday chores.

No girl would ever think to cover herself,
or flee to safety amidst men.
The boys preoccupied with being young
would at most hail her beauty
but they wouldn't dare touch her,
if they were interested
in being members of the community,

Inversions do creep in
especially under the barrel of a gun.
The oppressor always makes his ways
the height of civilisation.
What was ordinary day attire
suddenly became nudity,
or insignia of the uneducated.
What was men hard at work,
Became sweaty studs longing for
their time to play.

TAKE ME TO THE FRONTLINE STATES

Mother is dead
I can't go home

Take me to the threshold
Of the land I call home
Take me to the frontline states

Maybe once I am there
The sight of care-free toddler
Laughing and speeding though the fields
Will console me
So that those who deny me home
Can see me smiling
Instead of weeping

Take me to the frontline states
Maybe I will see the women
at work singing through the day
maybe in that humming I will remember

my mother's lullaby.

Take me back there

So my song can be carried by the wind

To the grave that dares to house my mother

And I back at her

Will sing

Sleep oh loved one

silently

Be planted there

I am coming

Political exiles could not come home to bury their loved ones. Miriam Makeba was in political exile for 31 years. In 1960, shortly after the Sharpeville Massacre, Makeba discovered that her passport had been revoked by the Apartheid South African government. She couldn't even attend her mother's funeral.[6]

---

[6] Miriam Makeba (2010), *South African History Online.* https://www.sahistory.org.za/people/miriam-makeba [accessed 13/08/2022].

VICTORY TROPHIES FOR INVADERS

Today we pay

To see treasures that once belonged to us

Treasures

Carved

Chiselled

Furnaced

Gilded

are now victory trophies for our invaders.

How they held up

the narrative of our barbarism

is still a wonder,

while displaying

complex beauties

our artifacts

sophisticated signs of the proud

people from whose hands they were fashioned

Today we have to beg

sit around diplomatic tables

just to get back

what belongs to us

MAMA-GIRL

When mama came home,
her humming tuned the house,
the coal stove was set,
till the walls perspired.
It was the kind of love,
hot
just about to boil,

I am still convinced
that her hemlines
were always tucked with goodies,
they seemed to appear
from nowhere,

I loved mama.
I got to see her once a week
or every two weeks.
When I found her home,
I knew that day home was complete.

I once went to where momma spent her days

away from us.

She lived in a dingy room,

right at the back,

I knew she lived there

because even that sorry hole

had ribbons that held the cupboard doors together.

Some little girl called her

by her name.

Not mama or Mrs?

Mavis!

I saw my queen

taking instructions from a child.

They kept my mama

for so long

I was jealous of them.

No

I hated them.

She was mama to me

but just a girl to them.

DON'T YOU TAKE THAT BOW

Don't you take that bow,
and plaque your pride on this work.
Don't let the privilege of carrying my tools,
fool you into thinking you contributed.

Don't walk in your black hood,
head high-up,
lying about your role in this work.
Tell them you dust the floors,
while we – the great ones – work.

This brilliance shall bear no black name,
it may suggest they too have a brain.
This applause doesn't have you in mind,
Don't you dare take that bow.

"Hamilton Naki was a black gardener who went on to work in the animal laboratory at the University of Cape Town and assisted Christian Barnard in the research effort that preceded the first human heart transplantation. Naki, who came from rural Transkei, had no access to higher education under apartheid. Yet, he developed excellent technical skills and, in *Hidden Heart*, Barnard is shown to have valued Naki's intraoperative role alongside his expertise at running the animal laboratory and in training a generation of future surgeons. According to interviews with Naki and Barnard in *Hidden Heart*, Naki was in the theatre during heart and liver transplant, which was illegal at that time because he was black—a claim that has been disputed."[7]

---

[7] Cristina Karrer, Werner Schweizer, *Hidden Heart: Hamilton Naki and Christiaan Barnard The True Story of the World's First Heart Transplant* (Swiss Films/Dschoint Ventschr Filmproduktion AG, 2008).

THOSE TAKEN

MY BABY GIRL

He can barely look at her,
too afraid to love her,
lest she is taken from him later.
He looks outward
and he begins to pray;

"As for you baby girl,
I do not know how your future will be,
but wherever it takes you,
know that somewhere deep inside of you,
though all things around you suggest otherwise,
you were made from the strongest elements
the universe has even known.

This is no false claim my baby girl,
we have survived capture
death marches paced by chains,
neck-to-neck,
limb-to-limb.

We know what it is like to walk and not look back,
and when we did look back,
it was just before we were lowered into the ship's belly.
My darling you will hear
about the valley of the shadow of death,
we have been there,
placed like spoons,
into the oceans lulled only by darkness.

You cry now,
I have heard the harrowing wailing,
of people dying with no comfort.
You will hear us sing often,
we started singing then,
to silence the weeping.
We've known the talker's silence,
and the realisation that the brother
or sister
liyng next to us,
has embraced death's eternal silence.

My baby girl

we've survived that,

and found ourselves on little stools,

inspected and traded.

We lost our names.

We belonged to someone who wasn't us.

We work day and night,

and those who get tired

fall on every side,

to be whipped back up on their feet,

and die

for us to bury them and move on.

Child

you are here now.

May all we have seen,

all that has happened to us,

Never descend upon you.
                        So I pray".

SHE WAS JUST A GIRL

She was just a girl
Riding on hopes of a better tomorrow
Still green
In need of bending and moulding

She knew little about her appearance
And how it could stand before her future
She was just a girl
Begging to sit and learn

Her small frame
Bright with her Sunday dress
Still needing wear
Colourful like fresh morning
And rhythms of song
As she walked into her learning

Just a little girl
Walked into tides of whiteness
Mercilessly crushing on her
She was no little girl

not just a girl

She was a black girl

Who dared to sit next to a white child

And learn at the same time

On November 14, 1960, at the age of six, Ruby Bridges became the first African American child to integrate an all-white elementary school in the South. In 1954, in a landmark case, Brown v. Board of Education, the Supreme Court ruled unanimously that racial segregation of children in public schools was unconstitutional. On the first day in her new school, Ruby and her mother arrived with four U.S. marshals for protection. There was a massive crowd of people shouting, throwing objects, and carrying signs as they approached the school. As soon as Ruby entered William Frantz Elementary, white families took their children out of the school. Ruby was routinely tormented on her way to school[8].

---

[8] Ruby Bridges, *Through My Eyes* (New York: Scholastic, 1999).

NATURAL INCREASE

Black bodies were the main domestic crop
An industry thriving
To build the very industries
they are excluded from today

In some twisted way
these precious bodies
were as precious as cargo
In the eyes of the enslavers

They forced intimacy
forced blacks to breed
And mix and match those whom they believed
Had the strongest constitution
To produce their super slave
Children made and taken

The livestock
The crop
The cargo

The currency

The commodity

Our people

"Slavers called slave-breeding "natural increase", Thomas Jefferson bragged to George Washington that the birth of black children was increasing Virginia's capital stock by four percent annually. Here is how the American slave-breeding industry worked, according to Sublette: some states (most importantly Virginia) produced slaves as their main domestic crop. The price of slaves was determined by the demand of industries in other states that consumed slaves in the production of rice and sugar, and by constant territorial expansion. As long as the slave power continued to grow, breeders could bank on future demand and increasing prices. That made slaves not just a commodity, but the closest thing to money that white breeders had.[9]

---

[9] Ned, Constance Sublette, *The American Slave Coast: A History of the Slave-Breeding Industry* (Brooklyn, New York: Lawrence Hill Books, 2015).

LET FREEDOM SING

For Marian Anderson

They didn't mind hearing you Marian,
when you dug deep into your contralto,
lifting them up high,
carrying them,
into sounds where birds harmonise,
with wings resting on the silent breeze.

When you stopped singing,
they were no longer lost in your sound,
and quickly remembered,
that you wore the black skin they would rather not see.

You lived the awkward paradox,
where the unwanted can be heard,
where the beautiful sounds are heard,
coming from bodies they would not show.
You could walk with kings,
be invited into gilded halls,

and yet have no decent place on which to lay your black head.

Even in your own country,

with your dignity,

all stupendous intonations,

they didn't let you sing in their Constitution Hall.

Yet, you stood to sing,

on an Easter Sunday

in nineteen thirty-nine,

Without a trace of malice or rage.

"My country, 'tis of thee,

Sweet land of liberty,

Of thee I sing;

Land where my fathers died,

Land of the pilgrims' pride,

From every mountainside

Let freedom ring!"

The Daughters of the American Revolution (DAR) had Marian Anderson barred from singing in Washington D.C.'s Constitution Hall because she was Black. It took First Lady Eleanor Roosevelt to help Anderson hold the concert at Lincoln Memorial, on federal property. The performance took place on Easter Sunday, April 9, 1939, and was attended by 75.000 people.[10]

---

[10] Susan Stamberg, Denied A Stage, She Sang For A Nation (2014) *NPR* https://www.npr.org/2014/04/09/298760473/denied-a-stage-she-sang-for-a-nation [accessed 11/02/2022].

OTA BENGA (1883 — 1916)

It was a twisted currency
Backed by no precious minerals
but by a more precious gem –
black lives

There was no brisk walking
in the lush fields
no rolling in the hay
no lone expeditions
that did not spell capture and enslavement

Such was the fate of so young a life
alone needing defence
walking right into the open claws
into open graves
snares of the slave traders

When the promise of freedom
seemed to turn his way
it was a charade

and for a measly pound of salt
a lousy bolt of cloth
he was bought from evil to evil

Benga was forcefully carved
Into a state of savagery
Along with animals
He was caged
Made a spectacle
A black beast
Captured from his kind
In the African jungle

When freedom finally came
He could not receive it
In thirty-three years
He knew no love
He longed for the Africa he could not get to
He could not recover from his pain
He could not take it anymore

"Ota Benga was born in the Congo in central Africa sometime around 1885. He was exhibited at the St. Louis World's Fair ("Louisiana Purchase Exhibition") in 1904 after being captured from his homeland. His tribe, the Batwa or Mbuti people, and his family were murdered by the violent Force Publique, the military force of the Belgian government. After being sold by slave traders, he ended up in the hands of businessman and white-supremacist Samuel Phillips Verner, who was under contract to bring back "pygmies" for exhibition at the St. Louis World Fair. Benga and eight other men were taken to America by Verner for the purposes of display and exploitation. Once they arrived at the fair, Benga and four of the other captives were placed on exhibition along with other Indigenous people of the Americas and Asia. Visitors were eager to see Ota Benga's teeth, which had been filed ritualistically into sharp points, and to see his small stature. He was advertised as a "cannibal," and the group was expected to behave savagely. When the public was not around, the men were measured and studied as scientific specimens by academics of the time, who were trying to prove the supremacy of people of European descent. Benga was placed in the American Museum of Natural History in New York City and after that his next destination was the Bronx Zoo in 1906. That September, he was placed on exhibit in the "Monkey House" with an orangutan. Prominent Black leaders pleaded with the mayor and with zoological societies to intervene. So much attention was drawn to

Benga that even the New York Times published an editorial denouncing his display. Eventually, African American clergymen were able to petition for his release. In late September 1906, after 20 days of exhibition, the zoo quietly removed Benga from display. Finally, in 1910, Benga was brought to Lynchburg, Virginia, where his teeth were capped and he attended school at the Virginia Theological Seminary and College (known today as Virginia University of Lynchburg). His loneliness became unbearable. On the night of March 20, 1916, Benga removed the caps from his teeth and built a ceremonial fire. His young friends watched as he danced and chanted around the flames in a ritual unknown to them. Later that night Benga ended his own life with a pistol shot through the heart. He was only about 30 years old."[11]

---

[11] Emily Kubota, Ota Benga Mbye Otabenga (2021) *The Lynchburg Museum* https://www.lynchburgmuseum.org/blog/2021/8/9/ota-benga-mbye-otabenga cited 21/06/2023 [accessed 20/11/2023].

RHINELAND BASTARDS

Round them up

And let them join our ranks

Let them swell our trenches

And fight with us

Let them believe this war

Is also their problem

They have stationed in the Rhineland

No longer far from our people

They mingle

they love and are loved

Negro blood on the Rhine, the heart of Europe

The negrofied Rhine must not grow

Round them up

End their future

Abort the unborn

Render the fertile barren

Rhineland Bastards was a term used in Germany to describe Afro-Germans who were children of African soldiers (who fought with the French Army). They were stationed in the Rhineland during the occupation by France after World War I. This term was also used during Nazi Germany for other mixed-race people. In 1933 under the law of Prevention of Hereditary Diseased Offspring many mixed-race children and persons were sterilised to prevent future procreation and reproduction.[12]. On the topic, see the powerful movie *Where Hands Touch*, starring Amanda Stenberg.

---

[12] Lambert M. Surhone, Miriam T. Timpledon, Susan F. Marseken (eds), *Rhineland Bastard* (Riga: VDM Publishing, 2010).

FOR SARAH BAARTMAN

I watched him come to me

Talking to me gently

Selling a place where I might attempt to live a dignified life

I've known some pain

But Nothing compared to this degradation

They poked my body with sticks

Like some creature foreign to humanity

They caged me

Placed me in public squares to jeer at me

Stripped my personhood bare

Claimed my normalities were abnormal

In their crooked mind

This is an affirmation that

My kind

are beasts of the wild

while they are superior

I think of home
Where normal exists,
pure normal,
the only luxury I yearn for
My being is spent as a tool of exhibition
And everyday I realise that home is but a dream
That I could die here
That I am going to die here

In my mind's eye
Everyday
I long to see the day
Where my warrior people will come for me.
Days turn to months
Months to years
Until…
I hear as my spirit hovers
my name being called
And my body being gathered again

I am going home
To be normal again
and on those silent valleys

with my own I shall dance

I am home.

Sarah 'Saartjie' Baartman was born in 1789 in Eastern Cape province of South Africa. She belonged to the Khoikhoi tribe. On 29 October 1810, Sarah allegedly 'signed' a contract with an English ship surgeon named William Dunlop. Apparently, the terms of her 'contract' were that she would travel with Hendrik Cezar and Dunlop to England and Ireland to work as a domestic servant and be exhibited for entertainment purposes. Sarah Baartman's large buttocks and unusual colouring made her the object of fascination by Europeans. She was taken to London where she was displayed, half naked, in a cage at a building in Piccadilly. In September 1814, she was taken to France and sold to Reaux, a man who showcased animals. He exhibited her in a cage alongside a baby rhinoceros. Often Sarah would be displayed completely naked and was nicknamed "Hottentot Venus". March 1815 Sarah was studied by French anatomists, zoologists and physiologists and it was concluded that she was the link between animals and humans. Sarah Baartman died in 1816, in Paris, at the age of 26. Her remains were dissected and eplaced in preserve bottles and then displayed in the Paris Museum of Man. In 2002 her remains returned to South Africa to be buried in her ancestral land, the Gamtoos Valley in the Eastern Cape.[13]

---

[13] C. Clifton, P. Scully, *Sara Baartman and the Hottentot Venus: A Ghost Story and a Biography* (United States of America: Princeton University Press, 2010) pp. 1-39.

TULSA

It was as if they had swallowed a thorn,

every time they passed Greenwood,

it stabbed them from within,

that blacks were moving on,

living happily,

carrying on with their lives -

thriving.

Waiting,

stalking like hunters in the wild,

they hoped for one break,

that unfortunate day,

a young man

remembered that black error

has no forgiveness,

it is a death trap,

a chase,

whose ultimate victory

is the public killing of the prey.

Then the inferno began,
their happy moment,
licenced the terror,
the killing,
the burning,
the end of the Black Wall Street.

Outrage?
No.
Reverential silence across the land,
after all nothing new had happened,
it was just black lives,
black livelihood.
Vanquished.

The Tulsa race massacre of 1921 is one of the most severe incidents of racial violence in American history. It occurred in Tulsa, Oklahoma, beginning on May 31, 1921, and lasted for two days. The massacre left between 30 and 300 people dead, mostly African Americans, and destroyed Tulsa's prosperous Black neighbourhood of Greenwood, known as the "Black Wall Street." More than 1,400 homes and businesses were burned, and nearly 10,000 people were left homeless.[14]

---

[14] Carole Boston Weatherford, *Unspeakable: The Tulsa Race Massacre* (Minneapolis: Lerner Publishing Group, 2021).

ANTI-BLACK PHILOSOPHERS

Do you go back and sit

at the feet of someone who

did not believe in your humanity?

The "thought leader",

who reduces your people,

your identity,

your very self?

The much-celebrated Immanuel Kant

could not miss placing his kind

at the top of perfection;

"Humanity is at its greatest perfection in the race of the whites".

David Hume:

"I am apt to suspect the Negroes,

and in general all other species of men ... to be naturally inferior to the whites."

Friedrich Hegel:

"Africa is no historical part of the world; it has no movement or development to exhibit".

After all this
even now Africans
must contend with the question
of whether African philosophy
exists or not.
As if to suggest that Africans
are unable to contemplate
life's deep questions.

Do we go back
to read these racists?

BRING HIM HOME

Prince Dejatch Alemayehu

The baby prince's wailing

can be heard in his homeland – Ethiopia.

He can't rest in perfect peace.

He was taken.

He died while away.

His people are unsettled.

They ask please bring him home,

Let him rest with his own.

His remains – trapped in English grounds.

and the English won't let him go.

> "The story of how a young Ethiopian prince came to be buried more than 5.000 miles from his East African home in Britain's Windsor Castle is still reverberating today, with Buckingham Palace under pressure after refusing to return his remains, and Britain once again being forced to reckon with its colonial past"[15].

---

[15] Adela Suliman, Why Buckingham Palace won't return a 'stolen' Ethiopian prince's remains (2023) *Washington Post*

IMAN

If the nose isn't wide

and the lips plump

If the cheek bones are high

And her face chiselled

If everything seems to be in its place

Then

It isn't black

If it is black

Then it is a white woman

Dipped in chocolate

In a 1979 article, Marcia Ann Gillespie, the then editor-in-chief of Essence Magazine referred to the black model Iman, in writing, as "a white woman dipped in chocolate".

---

https://www.washingtonpost.com/history/2023/05/23/ethiopia-prince-alemayehu-windsor-castle/ [accessed 23/05/2023].

TODAY

EVEN UNSAID IT STILL IS

Two persons in one

act harmoniously

as they give way to each other,

to display the desired character,

as the audience demands.

Smile...

This is body progressive,

inclusive speaking...

hugging

touching

comforting

chanting

"We are one human race!"

Frown...

In private,

it speaks truthfully;

"blacks,

are inferior,

are loud

stupid

savages

and are taking over"

isn't it interesting
that today you can't find
whites who supported Apartheid?

Yet
their minds have not changed
their hearts still pump hatred
only this time,
they are quiet
and offer us their public face.

Their private thoughts
seep through the cracks of their
high-walled homes,
as they speak free
where blacks are not around.

COLOURISM

Tell me earth does not glow

Nor chocolate shimmer

Tell me velvet rests not on skin

That too dark too black

Knows no beauty

Point me to the dunes

And tell me they're a little brighter

Than milk and whisper

You can get that light

They scorn and tell us that our brown skin

Is a hundred degrees low

Compared to white skin

Then sell us the paste to make us bright

Then bright and pale

Then red with pain

And aches at the sight of beauty gambled

And humming of old right true

"the blacker the berry, the sweeter the juice".

BAN THE BLACK MAN

Belinda Migor

Took what is normal private white banter

And put it on a public forum;

"Ban the black man

They rape

They steal

Worse than any Pitbull could do

And they get away with it.

Ban those that are making the laws

Ban Ekurhuleni

Ban the black man

Get all the black women

Cut out the uteruses and ovaries

So that they cannot procreate

Because they'll all turn out the same

Because they're all the same

I am very passionate about this

Ban them

Kill them

Shoot them

Get rid of them

Because they are the problem

Not pitbulls

Not animals

Animals are beautiful

They deserve a warm bed

Food

Love

And attention

And everything else

God created them

Who created the black man?

Do you think it was God?

I don't think so"

Belinda Migor left a voice note in a community group where she expressed her preference for dogs over black people. There were many cases of children and adults being mauled to death by pitbulls in South Africa, and some were calling for a ban or restrictions on this breed of dogs as domestic pets. November 2022, South Africa.

AMERICA

Today

In America

A black man

Cannot walk freely

Without it being

Extreme sport

First

He must look

As ordinary as possible

Preferably

As learned as possible

Just to show

That he is no thug

Once he is outside

He must pray he will find no police on his path

If he does

He must first lift his hands

And do exactly as he is told

One move

Even a twitch

And he could be dead

FLOYD

We've been suffocating,

for thousands of years.

The gallows here south

know the silencing

of our kind.

Even there

up northwest,

they've lynched our people,

and left them like

demonic scare crows

to scare us into silence.

You Floyd

were poured out like libation,

and your pleas

to be spared

were like harrowing prayers,

until

you evoked your mother's name.

What were you to do?

Children cry to and for their mothers,
they are crying for home,
for peace,
for love.

Old tears that still run today.
Our streets are still gallows,
where we die,
Slaughtered mercilessly.

UKRAINE

In Ukraine

after the Russia's invasion

White women and children

Were given priority

On transport leaving the country

African women and children

Were prevented from boarding

Even though there were empty seats

Kyiv, February 2022

THE BEAUTIFUL GAME

Romelu Lukaku

They call it -
    "The Beautiful Game"
        until someone throws a banana at you.

On Tuesday the 4th of April 2023, Juventus fans in Turin made racist remarks towards Romelu Lukaku: "Monkey chants could be heard from some sections of the Juventus fans. Other fans chanted in Italian the equivalent of f*** off' and 'f***ing monkey."[16]

---

[16] Phil Spencer, Romelu Lukaku sent off after hushing Juventus fans following monkey chants with abuse described as 'beyond despicable (2023) *Talk Sport* https://talksport.com/football/1385226/romelu-lukaku-juventus-inter-milan-chelsea/ [accessed 4/07/2023].

BLACK THUG

My pants are loaded
With clean money
From my own sweat

I clean my black frame
Then ironed my shirt and trousers
Perfectly framing my shoulders
Sharpening the lines
From my waist down to the floor

I walk the streets
With bounce and swag
And hear my folks
Cheering at me saying -
"Hey chocolate boy
Where you going so fine?"

It's my day to pay myself back
For even the holy book says
A workman need not be ashamed

I hit the town

I know my style

I know what I want

As soon as I step into that shop

They follow me everywhere

Waiting for me to steal

COVID: THEY DIDN'T FORGET

The whole human race,
faced the same struggle
in some tragic twisted way,
it was an opportunity
to stand as one.

Yet in the depths of a global threat,
some did not forget
to prioritise themselves;

"Let remedy find them last.
Lock them out.
Let them stay in, far from us".

They remembered that we are less
even amidst global suffocation,
they closed Africans out.

REFERENCES

Adela Suliman, Why Buckingham Palace won't return a 'stolen' Ethiopian prince's remains (2023) *Washington Post* https://www.washingtonpost.com/history/2023/05/23/ethiopia-prince-alemayehu-windsor-castle/ [accessed 23/05/2023].

Baroness Lola Young, The hidden history of the sinking of the SS Mendi (2014) *British Council* https://www.britishcouncil.org/voices-magazine/hidden-history-sinking-ss-mendi [accessed 20/10/2023].

C. Clifton, P. Scully, *Sara Baartman and the Hottentot Venus: A Ghost Story and a Biography* (Princeton: Princeton University Press, 2010).

Carole Boston Weatherford, *Unspeakable: The Tulsa Race Massacre* (Minneapolis: Lerner Publishing Group, 2021).

Cristina Karrer, Werner Schweizer, *Hidden Heart: Hamilton Naki and Christiaan Barnard The True Story of the World's First Heart Transplant* (Swiss Films/Dschoint Ventschr Filmproduktion AG, 2008).

Emily Kubota, Ota Benga Mbye Otabenga (2021) *The Lynchburg Museum* https://www.lynchburgmuseum.org/blog/2021/8/9/ota-benga-mbye-otabenga cited 21/06/2023 [accessed 20/11/2023].

Lambert M. Surhone, Miriam T. Timpledon, Susan F. Marseken (eds), *Rhineland Bastard* (Riga: VDM Publishing, 2010).

Martin Ewans, *European Atrocity, African Catastrophe: Leopold II, the Congo Free State and Its Aftermath* (London: Routledge, 2002).

Miriam Makeba (2010), *South African History Online* https://www.sahistory.org.za/people/miriam-makeba [accessed 13/08/2022].

Ned, Constance Sublette, *The American Slave Coast: A History of the Slave-Breeding Industry* (Brooklyn, New York: Lawrence Hill Books, 2015).

Overcoming Apartheid, Building Democracy, (2005), Michigan State University https://overcomingapartheid.msu.edu/multimedia.php?kid=163-582-18 [accessed 17/02/2023].

Phil Spencer, Romelu Lukaku sent off after hushing Juventus fans following monkey chants with abuse described as 'beyond despicable (2023) *Talk Sport* https://talksport.com/football/1385226/romelu-lukaku-juventus-inter-milan-chelsea/ [accessed 4/07/2023].

Ruby Bridges, *Through My Eyes* (New York: Scholastic, 1999).

Susan Stamberg, *Denied A Stage, She Sang For A Nation* (2014) *NPR* https://www.npr.org/2014/04/09/298760473/denied-a-stage-she-sang-for-a-nation [accessed 11/02/2022].

The story of Sarah Baartman and the poem 'I've come to take you home. https://socialjustice.sun.ac.za/downloads/events/2022-10-diana-ferrus-on-sarah.pdf. [accessed 20/10/2023].

Thomas Pakenham, *The Scramble for Africa* (London: Abacus Little Brown Book Group, 2015).

www.ingramcontent.com/pod-product-compliance
Lightning Source LLC
Chambersburg PA
CBHW070849160426
43192CB00012B/2368